ELEPHANT
COLORING BOOK

Get FREE printable coloring pages and discounted book prices sent straight to your e-mail inbox every week!

Sign up at:

www.adultcoloringworld.net

PREVIEWS:

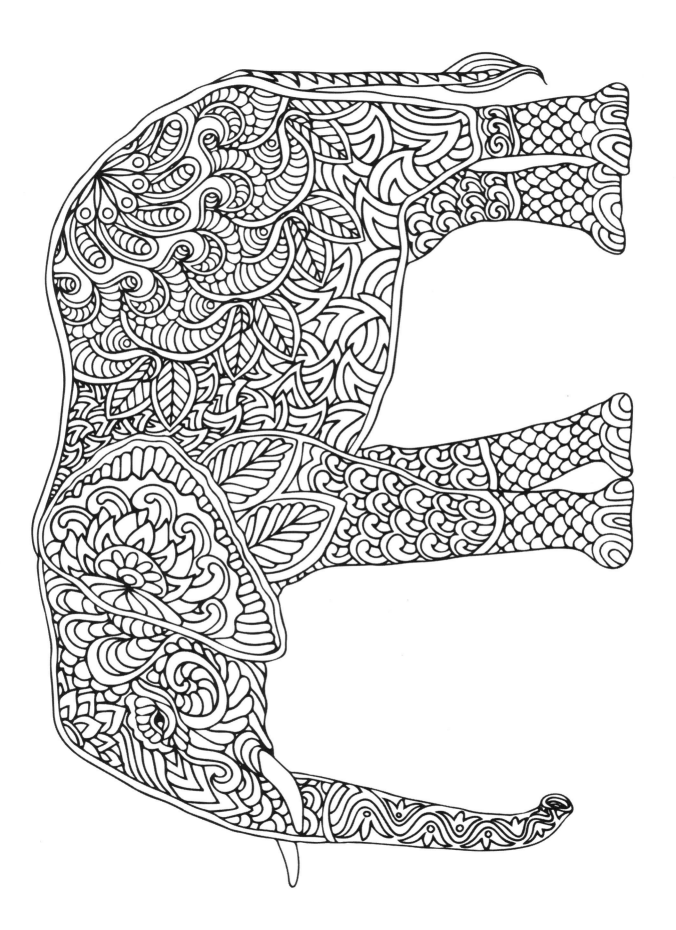

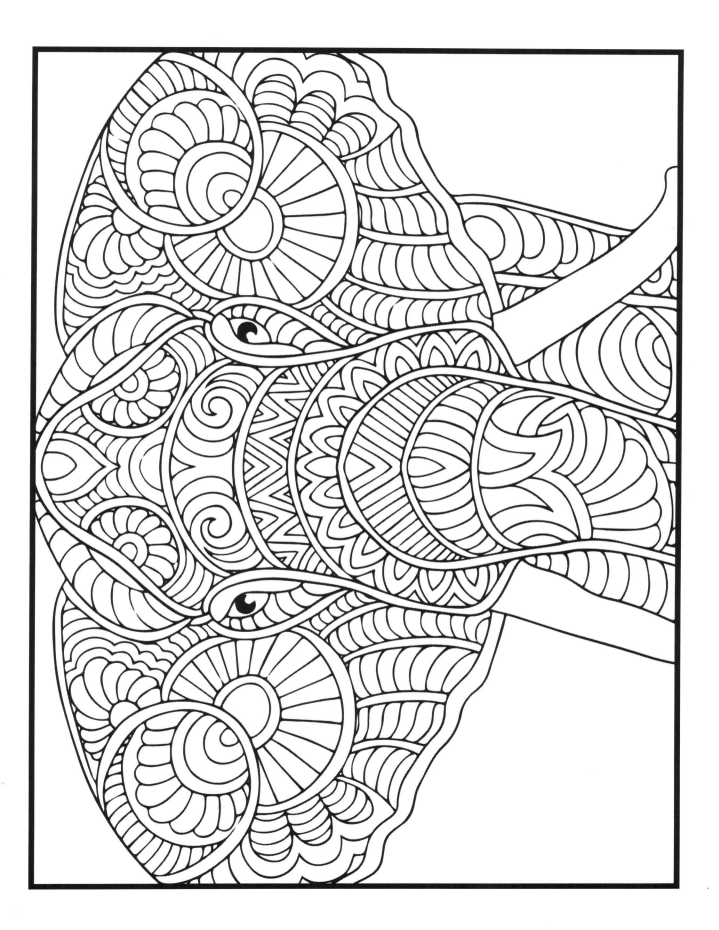

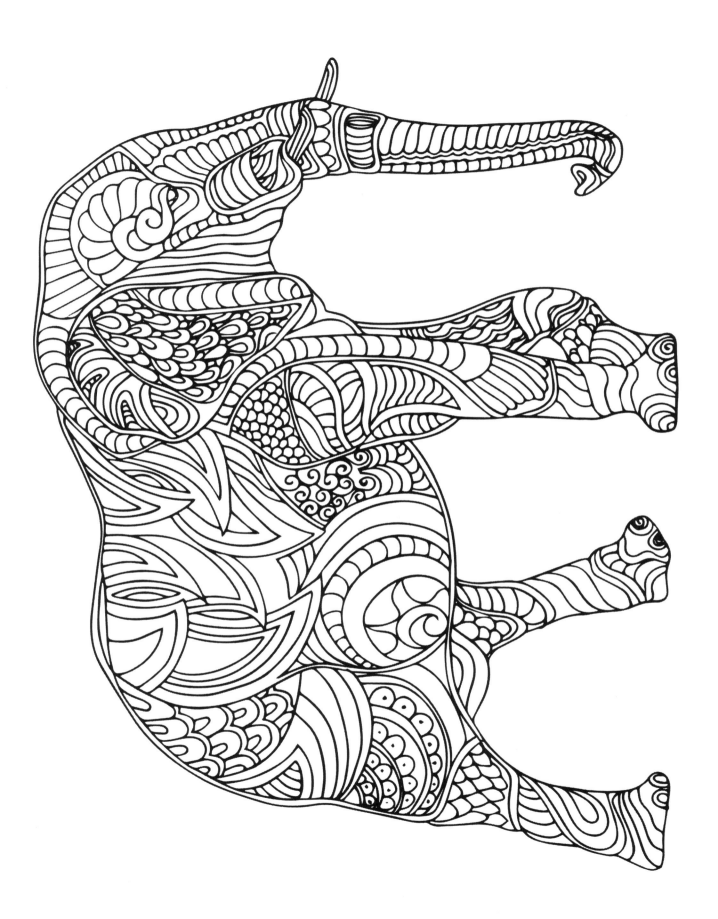

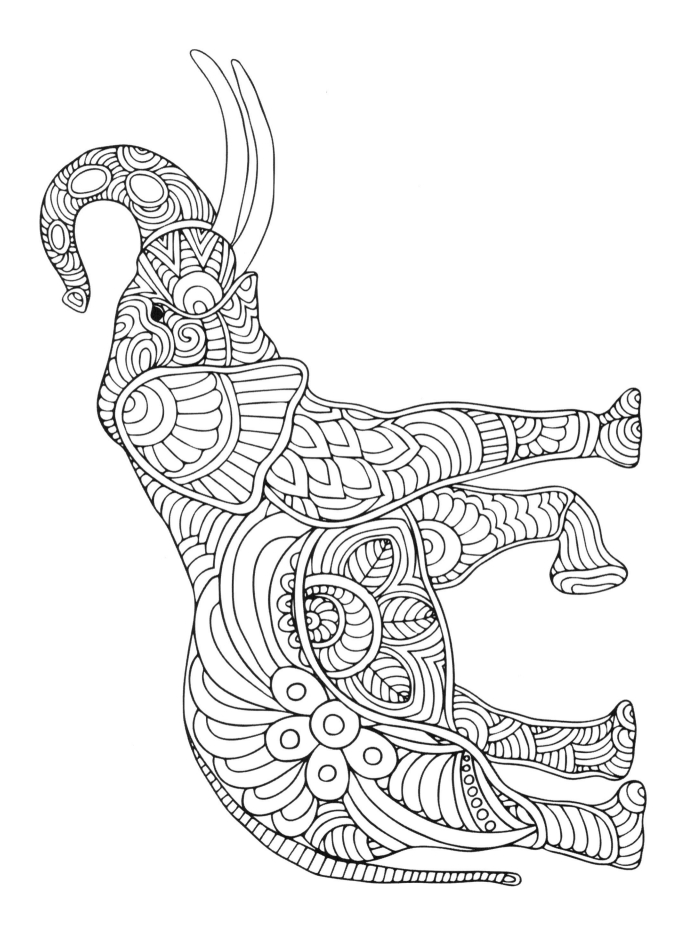

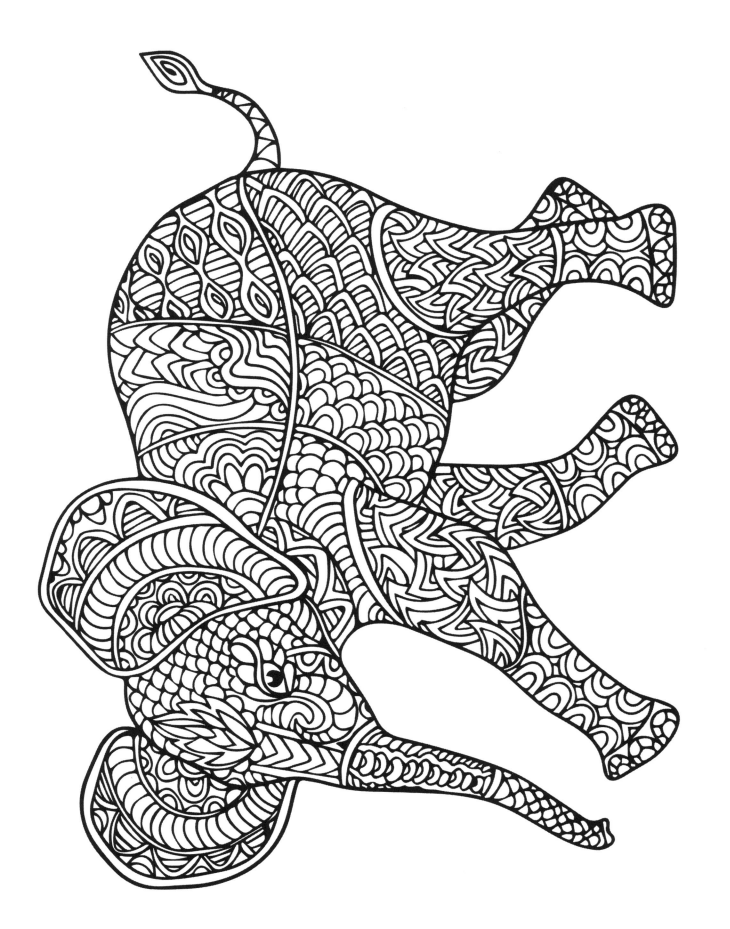

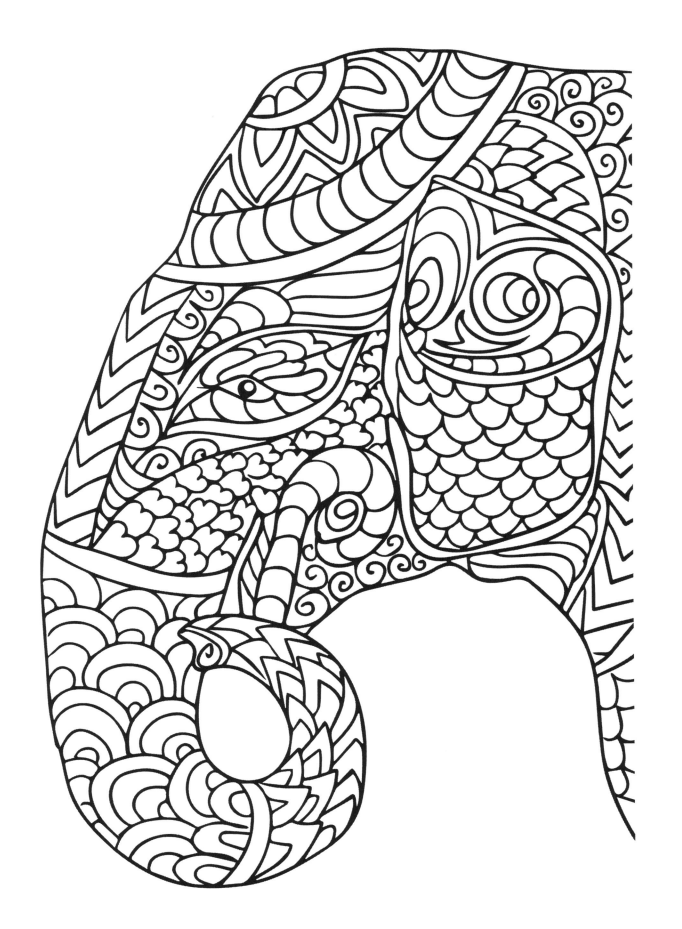

COLOR TEST PAGE

COLOR TEST PAGE

Made in the USA
Columbia, SC
04 June 2018